Place baby's photo here.

This album belongs to

....

Life before you

There was once a mother and a father (that's us!)
who loved each other very much.
So much that you already existed in our hearts.
We knew that you would arrive one day. . . .

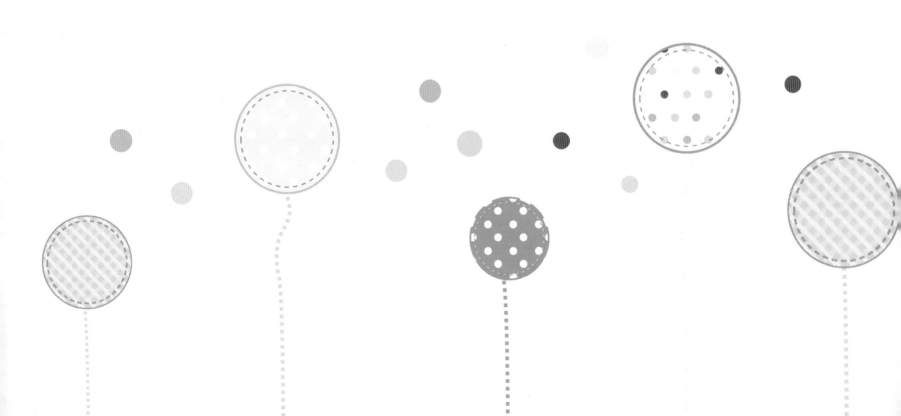

Even before we knew you were on the way, we thought of you often.
Here's how we imagined you:

....

....

....

....

....

....

....

....

....

Mom

My name is: ....

I was born on: ....

in: ....

Here are some of my favorite memories from before you were born:

....

....

....

....

....

....

....

....

Dad

My name is: ....

I was born on: ....

in: ....

Here are some of my favorite memories from before you were born:

....

....

....

....

....

....

....

....

....

....

....

....

....

....

Here are pictures of the two of us, Mom and Dad,
before you were born.

Brothers and sisters . . .

. . . all looking forward to your arrival!
They are so excited to welcome you.

Their name(s) and age(s) when you were born: ....

....

....

....

Place photos of brothers and sisters here.

Your family tree

Your father, your mother, your brothers and sisters—
oh, this is happiness!

Here is the family tree of your closest relatives.

Grandpa	Grandma		Grandpa	Grandma
....	....		....	....

Dad	Mom
....	....

You

....

Announcing your arrival

In an instant, our lives were changed forever.
You would be arriving in just nine months.

The most beautiful adventure of our lives had just begun,
thanks to you!

A few words from Mom

When I found out I was pregnant . . .

....

....

....

And when I shared this great joy with your dad . . .

....

....

....

....

....

....

....

....

....

....

....

....

....

....

....

....

Preparing for your arrival

Little by little, we have picked out onesies,
stuffed animals, and more to welcome you . . .
Your brother(s) and sister(s) also have things to share with you.
Here's how we made a place for you in our home.

This is the list of what we bought for you:

_____
_____
_____
_____
_____
_____
_____
_____

We made a lot of improvements at home!

_____
_____
_____
_____
_____
_____
_____
_____

So many things for such a little baby . . .

_____
_____
_____
_____
_____
_____
_____
_____
_____

Place a photo of preparing for baby's arrival here.

Your baby shower

Family and friends all came together to celebrate your anticipated arrival. Here are some of our favorite memories from that special day:

....

....

....

....

....

....

....

....

....

....

....

....

Place photos from the
baby shower here.

Your name

After endless debates, here is a list of names
we agreed upon:

....

....

....

....

....

....

....

Mom's
favorite names

Dad's
favorite names

Your first pictures

Two little feet, ten little fingers, a beating heart . . .
This is the story of seeing you for the first time.
Dad said you looked like him already!
. . . and Mom was so proud to carry you.

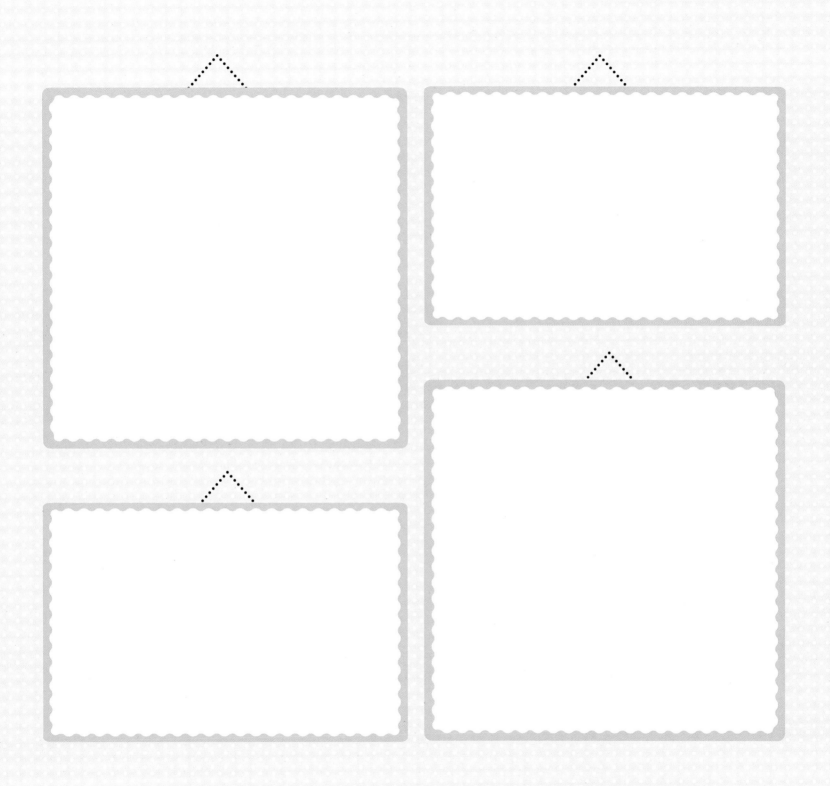

Here are your ultrasounds and photos of Mom's growing belly.

Getting your room ready

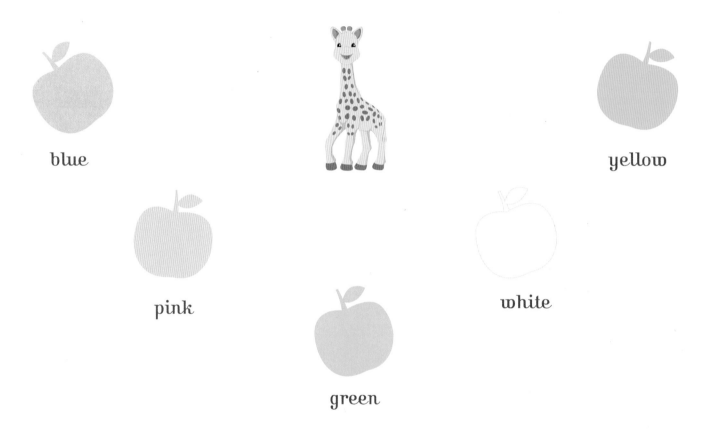

blue

yellow

pink

white

green

We have created a space just for you.
A crib, changing table, dresser . . .
Our home is yours now, too!

Here is a picture of your room.

You are finally here!

Your name:

....

You were born on:

....

At:

....

Where:

....

Your birth weight and length:

....

Our very first
impression of you:

....
....
....
....
....
....
....

Your hair color:

....

Your eye color:

....

Place baby's hospital bracelet here.

What a beautiful baby!

Place baby's first photo here.

Your first handprint

Your first footprint

Family resemblance

"She looks just like her grandmother!"
"He's the spitting image of his father. . . ."
Everyone has a point of view.
When you were born, you looked a lot like:

....

But also like: ....

....

....

....

....

....

....

Place family photos here.

You were born under a lucky star

The date and time of your birth have marked our lives forever.
But perhaps they may also influence your personality?

Your zodiac sign is:

....

Stubborn as a Taurus? Calm as an Aquarius?
Playful as a Gemini?
So far we have found you to be . . .

....

....

....

A year like no other

These are some of the major events that took place
around the time of your birth.

....
....
....
....
....
....
....

The front page of the newspaper on the day of your birth

Finally at home!

Bringing you home was a joyous event.
What an unforgettable day!

The reactions of the
whole family:

....

....

....

....

And what was your reaction
to your home?

....

....

....

....

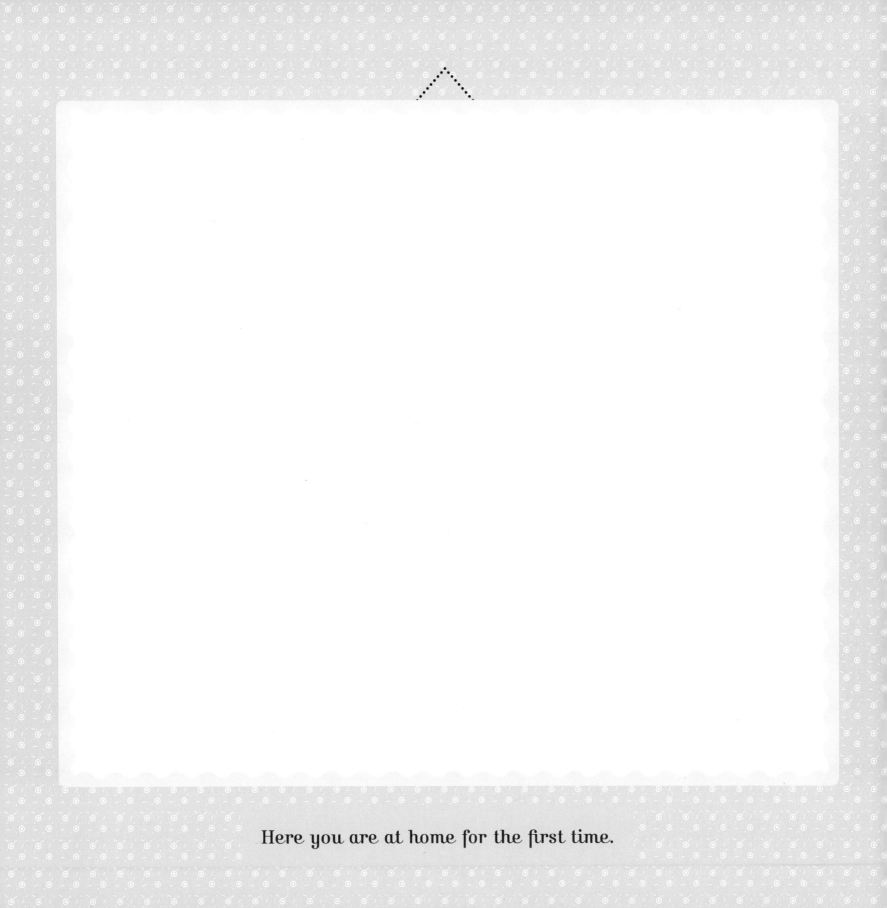

Here you are at home for the first time.

Your first visits!

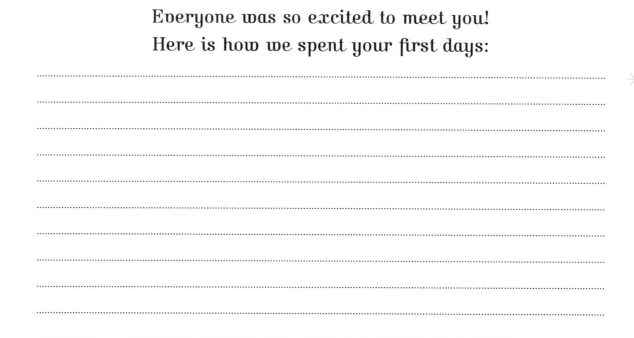

Everyone was so excited to meet you!
Here is how we spent your first days:

....

....

....

....

....

....

....

....

....

We received many visitors and gifts for you, including:

Your birth announcement

We snapped a few photos,
created a keepsake card, and voilà!
We were ready to announce your arrival to the world.

Special delivery!

Who gave you
your first bath?

....

....

....

....

....

Your reactions:

....

....

....

....

....

....

....

Here you are in
the bath!

Place a photo
of baby's first bath
here.

A day in the life

Between visits, walks, hugs, and feedings . . .
you are one busy baby!
Here's how you spend your days and nights.

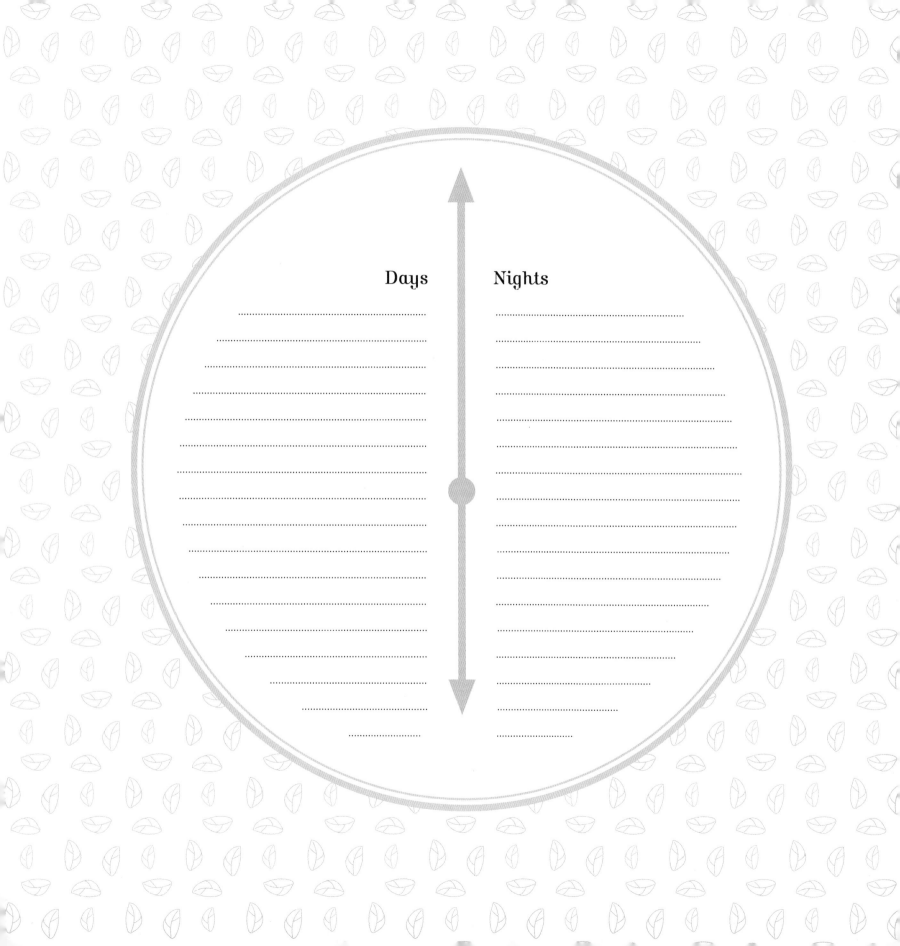

Days   Nights

They are here to watch over you

Here is your godmother.

Place a photo of baby's godmother here.

Here is your godfather.

Place a photo of baby's godfather here.

So many firsts

You are discovering the world,
and you're in awe.
We are so happy to see you open your eyes
to your surroundings!

Your first smiles: ....
....

Your first babblings: ....
....

The first time you sat up by yourself: ....
....
....

The first time you waved bye-bye: ....
....
....

The first time you made us laugh: ....
....
....

The first time you rolled over: ....
....

When you discovered your hands and feet: ....
....
....

First memories with you

Your first lock of hair

So many firsts, captured in photographs.

Place photos here.

A spoon, a fork . . .

A spoon for Mom,
a spoon for Dad . . .
Mmm, it's delicious!
You're a true gourmet,
cheeks smeared with carrots!

Menu

How you behaved during your first meal: ....
....

Who fed you? ....

Dad by flying with his spoon, Mom with the choo-choo train, or you all by yourself . . . here is how you ate: ....
....
....

The foods you liked: ....
....

Those you hated: ....
....

Your most favorite food? ....

Our first vacation

Here is one of our sweetest earliest memories.
On the beach, at a hotel, or camping out, here's what we did on our
first family vacation.

Our destination: ....

The treasures that we brought in your suitcase:
....

Your mood during our trip:
....

Activities and outings you took part in:

....

....

....

Your favorite parts of the trip: ....

....

....

....

Family vacation memories

Place a souvenir photo here.

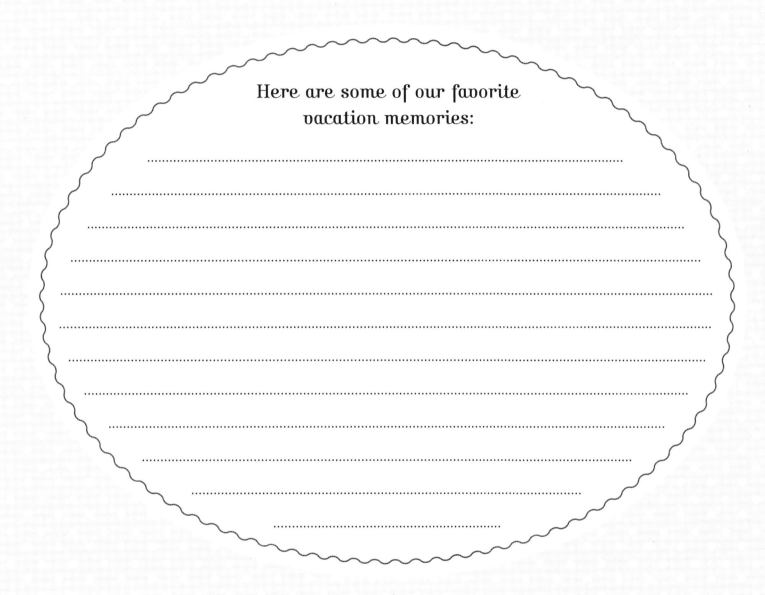

Here are some of our favorite
vacation memories:

....

....

....

....

....

....

....

....

....

....

....

Your first time with a babysitter

It's Mom and Dad's first night out in a long time. . . .
We were nervous to leave you, but it all turned out to be just fine.
Here's the story of your night:

....

....

....

....

....

....

....

Place a photo of baby sleeping here.

Your 1st birthday!

The whole family has gathered to shower you with love and gifts. Mom and Dad are so excited! We fondly remember the day you were born.

This is the story of your first birthday:

....

....

....

....

....

Your mountain of gifts:

....

....

....

....

....

....

....

....

What we feel on this special day:

....

....

....

....

....

Photos of your 1st birthday

Place photos of baby's first birthday here.

Place photos of baby's first birthday here.

Your favorite activities

There once was a little child who had just started to discover the surrounding world. Games, songs, animals, nature, and so much more!

Here are the things you like to do!

What are your
favorite games?

....

....

....

....

....

....

Who do you
love to play with?

....

....

....

....

....

....

What are your favorite
stories?

....

....

Who reads to you?

....

....

....

What is your favorite stuffed animal?

....

....

....

....

....

What are your favorite songs?

....

....

....

....

....

....

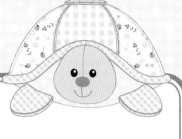

Who are your friends?

....

....

....

....

Place a picture of baby's friends here.

Your first steps

One foot in front of the other, to catch the ball or run into Mom's arms . . . today you walked like a big kid!

Some other memorable dates . . .

The first time you crawled: ....

The first time you stood up on

your own: ....

The first time you walked: ....

Your first holiday

The house is warm, bright, and full of family and friends.
We are all excited for you to open your presents. . . .

Here is the story of your first holiday:

....

....

....

....

....

....

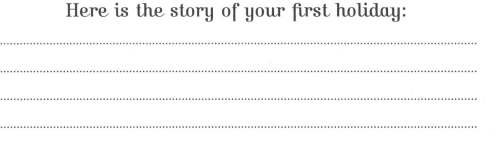

The gifts that you have received:

....

....

....

....

....

....

....

....

And even more:

....

....

....

....

....

....

Photos of your first holiday

Your first words

One day, a small miracle happened.
You talked, and it was wonderful!

Your first word:

....

When and where you said it:

....

Your first sentence:

....

When and where you said it:

....

Your funniest lines

As you learned to speak, you said some things that we will never forget! Some were cute, some wise beyond your years, and all of them memorable. . . .

You know how to make us laugh!

....
....
....
....
....
....
....
....
....
....

You are 2 years old,
you're growing up so fast!

Here is how we
celebrated your second birthday:

The Experiment, LLC
220 East 23rd Street, Suite 301
New York, NY 10010-4674
www.theexperimentpublishing.com

My Baby Album with Sophie la girafe was first published in 2012 by Marabout Editions as L'album de mon bébé avec Sophie la girafe ©. This revised and updated English-language edition is published by arrangement with Marabout.

The Experiment's books are available at special discounts when purchased in bulk for premiums and sales promotions as well as for fundraising or educational use. For details, contact us at info@theexperimentpublishing.com.

ISBN 978-1-61519-097-3

Text design by Marabout

Manufactured in China
Distributed by Workman Publishing Company, Inc.

First published September 2013
10 9 8 7 6